INCREDIBLE CREATURES OF THE Caribbean Sea

Learn About Animals Including Octopuses, Stingrays, Eels, and Triggerfish!

Amie Jane Leavitt

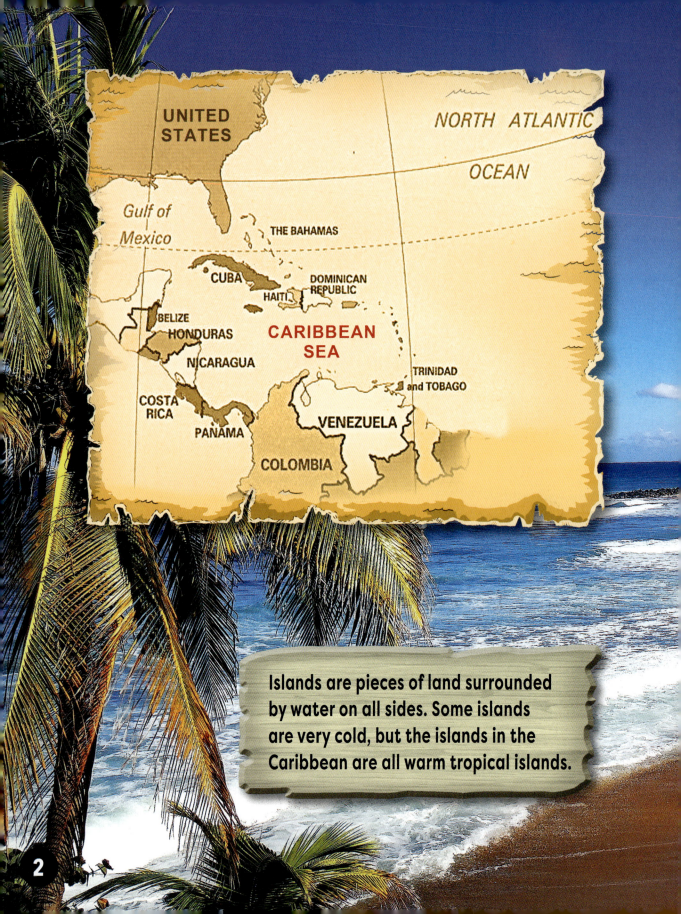

Islands are pieces of land surrounded by water on all sides. Some islands are very cold, but the islands in the Caribbean are all warm tropical islands.

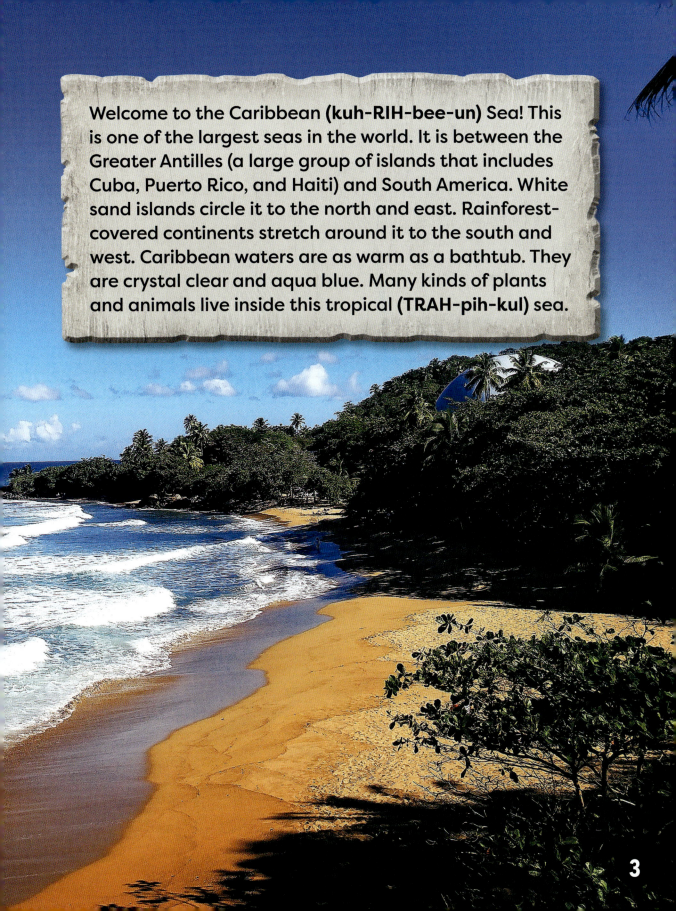

Welcome to the Caribbean **(kuh-RIH-bee-un)** Sea! This is one of the largest seas in the world. It is between the Greater Antilles (a large group of islands that includes Cuba, Puerto Rico, and Haiti) and South America. White sand islands circle it to the north and east. Rainforest-covered continents stretch around it to the south and west. Caribbean waters are as warm as a bathtub. They are crystal clear and aqua blue. Many kinds of plants and animals live inside this tropical **(TRAH-pih-kul)** sea.

The Caribbean Sea has the second largest coral reef (**KOR-ul REEF**) in the world. It stretches from Mexico to Honduras (**hahn-DUR-us**). Reefs are stony underwater walls. They are made by groups of small animals called corals.

Reefs look like a flower garden under the sea. The walls and the creatures that live there are mostly bright colors like blues, yellows, reds, and oranges. Tiny underwater plants called algae (**AL-jee**) give the walls their color. Sponges, fish, clams, and worms add to the colorful mix. Coral reefs are busy with life!

The Caribbean reef octopus hides and hunts all over the reef, changing colors and patterns to blend in with the background.

In the Caribbean, eels crawl in and out of coral caves. These sea creatures look like snakes, but they are actually a type of fish. The green moray eel can grow up to 8 feet (2.4 meters) long and weigh 65 pounds (29.5 kilograms). It keeps its mouth open to show its razor-sharp teeth.

Some reef animals, like the Christmas tree worm, look like flowers. They have feathery gills that are bright colors like red, orange, yellow, blue, or even purple.

The Atlantic goliath grouper isn't colorful like many of the other reef fish, but it still stands out because it's so big! These fish can grow over 8 feet (2.5 meters) long and can weight up to 800 pounds (362.9 kilograms).

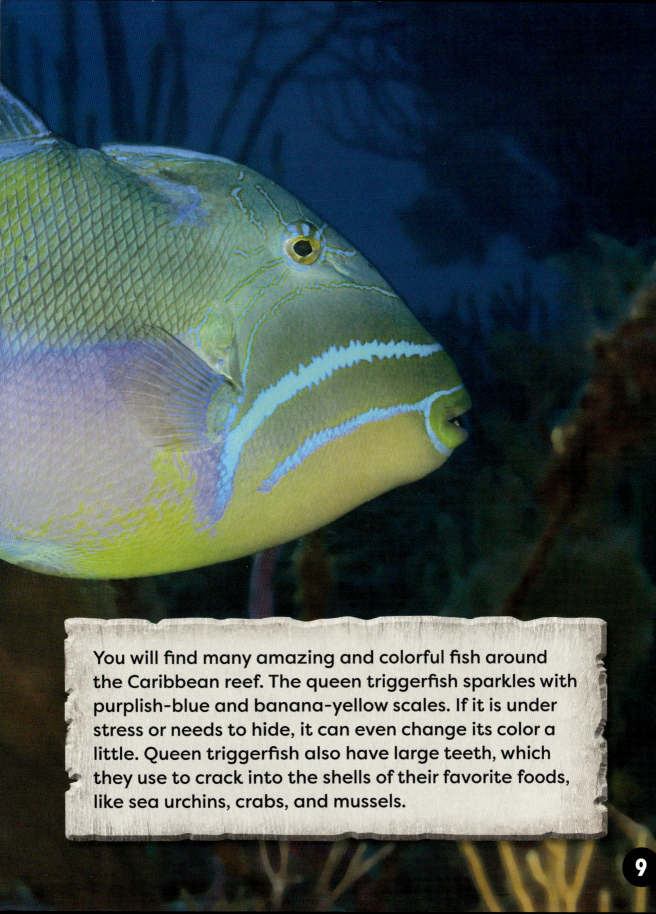

You will find many amazing and colorful fish around the Caribbean reef. The queen triggerfish sparkles with purplish-blue and banana-yellow scales. If it is under stress or needs to hide, it can even change its color a little. Queen triggerfish also have large teeth, which they use to crack into the shells of their favorite foods, like sea urchins, crabs, and mussels.

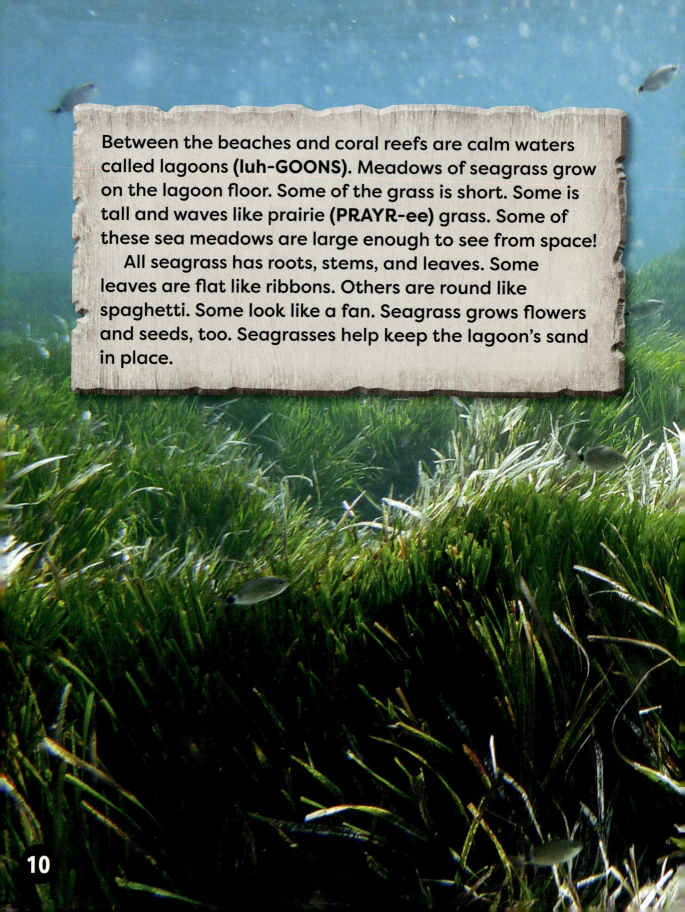

Between the beaches and coral reefs are calm waters called lagoons (**luh-GOONS**). Meadows of seagrass grow on the lagoon floor. Some of the grass is short. Some is tall and waves like prairie (**PRAYR-ee**) grass. Some of these sea meadows are large enough to see from space!

All seagrass has roots, stems, and leaves. Some leaves are flat like ribbons. Others are round like spaghetti. Some look like a fan. Seagrass grows flowers and seeds, too. Seagrasses help keep the lagoon's sand in place.

Green sea turtles graze on seagrass leaves. They are the only sea turtles that eat mostly plants as adults.

Seagrass gives animals a safe place to live, so it can be as lively and colorful as the coral reef. Pink shrimp and spiny lobsters hide in the meadow. Red cushion sea stars skim across the leaves. Green sea cucumbers that look a bit like large slugs slurp waste off the lagoon floor. These helpful animals keep everything neat and clean.

The queen conch (KONK) is a type of large sea snail that is recognized by it's large, spiral shell. These shells can grow to over 12 inches (30.5 centimeters) long. They thicken and develop flared lips as the animal gets older.

Hawksbill sea turtles are some of the most common sea turtles in the Caribbean Sea. The top part of their beak is longer and curves almost like a hawk's beak. They were the first reptiles found to be "biofluorescent," meaning that they seem to glow in certain types of light.

Hawksbill hatchlings are tiny, measuring less than 1 inch (2.5 centimeters) long and weighing less than 1 ounce (28.3 grams). They hatch at night and use light differences to find their way to the water.

Mangroves (MANG-grohvs) are trees that grow in salty water along tropical coastlines. Their roots reach up from the seabed to hold the trunk above water. Mangroves can survive in harsh places where other plants can't because they can filter salt and take in more oxygen.

Many birds like the scarlet ibis nest in the canopies of mangrove forests. These birds eat the crabs and shellfish that live in the shallow waters around the mangrove roots.

All kinds of creatures dwell among the mangrove roots. Fish and crabs dart in and out, while mussels, oysters, and barnacles fasten tight to the roots. They filter sand and silt out of the water. This helps keep the water clear.

Sea anemones (uh-NEH-moh-nees) might look like flowers, but they are really animals. In mangrove forests, they attach to the roots. Their stinging tentacles (TEN-tih-kuls) sway in the water like hair, protecting them and catching prey (PRAY).

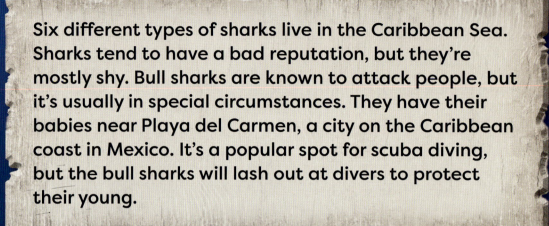

Six different types of sharks live in the Caribbean Sea. Sharks tend to have a bad reputation, but they're mostly shy. Bull sharks are known to attack people, but it's usually in special circumstances. They have their babies near Playa del Carmen, a city on the Caribbean coast in Mexico. It's a popular spot for scuba diving, but the bull sharks will lash out at divers to protect their young.

Nurse sharks are over 10 feet (3.1 meters) long. They are bottom dwellers that skirt along the ocean floor, eating small shellfish.

Squat lobsters look a bit like big bugs! In the Caribbean Sea, they usually live around deep-water coral. Since very little sunlight reaches that deep, they have very big eyes to help them see in the dark.

The Caribbean spiny lobster lives on the seafloor in shallow waters. They are most active at night and hide in crevices during the day. One of the most amazing things about Caribbean spiny lobsters is how they travel to avoid winter storms. They migrate single file as far as 31 miles (50 kilometers) to the deeper water that stays calmer during storms.

The scorpionfish (**SKOR-pee-un-fish**) lives on a seafloor that is filled with color. Its sunburst scales help it blend in and hide. Once hidden, it lies in wait, sneaking up on its prey. Scorpionfish have venom (**VEH-num**) in their spines to protect them from predators and stun prey if needed.

Scorpionfish have large mouths, which they use like a vacuum to quickly suck in food like fish and shrimp.

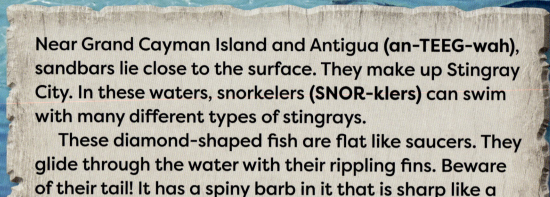

Near Grand Cayman Island and Antigua (an-TEEG-wah), sandbars lie close to the surface. They make up Stingray City. In these waters, snorkelers (**SNOR-klers**) can swim with many different types of stingrays.

These diamond-shaped fish are flat like saucers. They glide through the water with their rippling fins. Beware of their tail! It has a spiny barb in it that is sharp like a serrated knife and has venom inside.

Stingrays have their eyes on top of their bodies so that when they dig down into the sand to hunt, they can still see their prey. Behind their eyes, they have holes called "spiracles," which they use to breathe while hunting.

The world's largest fish loves the warm Caribbean Sea. It is the whale shark, and it can grow up to 42 feet (12.8 meters) long. That is almost as long as a school bus! A whale shark's eyeballs are covered in something called "dermal denticles," which are very tiny teeth that protect their eyes from harm.

From the coral reefs to the mangrove forests and the deep, deep blue, the Caribbean Sea has all kinds of colorful sea life. And there are still so many more animals and plants out there yet to find!

The whale shark has as many as 3,000 tiny teeth in its mouth, but it doesn't bite to eat. It gulps huge amounts of water into its mouth and uses filter plates to filter tiny plants and animals called plankton out, letting the water flow back into the sea.

FURTHER READING

Books

Hanes, Kathleen. *Seagrass Dreams: A Counting Book*. Lake Forest, CA: Seagrass Press, 2017.

Marsh, Laura. *National Geographic Readers: Sea Turtles*. Washington, D.C.: National Geographic Society, 2011.

Priddy, Roger. *Smart Kids: Coral Reef*. London: Priddy Books, 2014.

Skerry, Brian. *National Geographic Kids Chapters: The Whale Who Won Hearts: And More True Stories of Adventures with Animals*. Washington, D.C.: National Geographic Society, 2014.

Web Sites

The Caribbean Reefs Guide
   https://reefguide.org/carib/

The Florida Museum of Natural History: Life in Seagrasses
   https://www.floridamuseum.ufl.edu/southflorida/habitats/seagrasses/life/

GLOSSARY

algae (AL-jee)—Small plants that grow in the water.

Antigua (an-TEEG-wah)—An island in the Caribbean Sea where stingrays live near sandbars.

conch (KONK)—A type of medium to large sea snail.

coral reef (KOR-ul REEF)—Stony wall made by an animal called coral.

filter (FIL-ter)—To act like a screen by letting water through and blocking or trapping dirt, food, and other things.

Honduras (hahn-DUR-us)—Country in Central America that contains a portion of the second largest coral reef in the Caribbean Sea.

lagoon (luh-GOON)—An area of usually shallow water that is separated from deeper water by a coral reef.

mangroves (MANG-grohvs)—Trees that grow in salty water along tropical coastlines.

prairie (PRAYR-ee)—Large open grassland.

prey (PRAY)—An animal that is hunted for food.

scorpionfish (SKOR-pee-un-fish)—A marine fish that lives on the seafloor and blends in with the colorful coral reefs to hide and sneak up on prey.

snorkeler (SNOR-kler)—A person who swims under the water while breathing through a tube that reaches above the water.

tentacle (TEN-tih-kul)—A flexible limb on an animal.

tropical (TRAH-pih-kul)—From the warm part of the earth that is near the equator.

venom (VEH-num)—A poison produced by certain animals, such as moray eels and stingrays.

PHOTO CREDITS

pp. 4-5—Shutterstock/Allexxandar; p. 5 (inset)—Shutterstock/John A. Anderson; pp. 6-7—Shutterstock/Imagine Earth Photography; p. 6 (inset)—Shutterstock/Drew McArthur; p. 7 (inset)—Shutterstock/Vietnam photo; pp. 8-9—Shutterstock/bearacreative; p. 8 (inset)—Shutterstock/Richard W. Eaker; p. 11 (inset)—Shutterstock/Rich Carey; pp. 12-13, 18-19—Shutterstock/Damsea; p. 13 (inset)—Shutterstock/orgbluewater; pp. 14-15—Shutterstock/Adam Leaders; p. 15 (inset)—Shutterstock/Bigc Studio; p. 17 (inset)—Shutterstock/Nandani Bridglal; pp. 20-21—Shutterstock/Carlos Grillo; pp. 22-23—Shutterstock/MYP Studio; p. 22 (inset)—Shutterstock/Kendo Nice; pp. 24-25—Shutterstock/Richard Whitcombe; pp. 26-27—Shutterstock/Matt Murph; p. 27 (inset)—Eric Carlander; p. 29 (inset)—Shutterstock/Wonderful Nature. All other photos—Public Domain.

INDEX

Algae 4
Anemones 19
Antigua 26
Atlantic goliath grouper 8
Bull sharks 20–21
Caribbean spiny lobster 22–23
Christmas tree worm 7
Coral reefs 4–7, 10, 12, 28
Eels 6
Grand Cayman Island 26
Greater Antilles 3
Green sea cucumbers 12
Green sea turtles 11
Hawksbill sea turtles 14–15
Honduras 4
Lagoons 10–11
Mangroves 16–19, 28
Mexico 4, 20
Nurse sharks 21
Octopus 5
Plankton 29
Playa del Carmen, Mexico 20
Queen conch 13
Queen triggerfish 8–9
Rainforest 3
Scarlet ibis 17
Scorpionfish 24–25
Sea stars 12–13
Seagrass 10–13
South America 3
Squat lobsters 22
Stingray City 26
Stingrays 26–27
Whale sharks 28–29

© 2025 by Curious Fox Books™, an imprint of Fox Chapel Publishing Company, Inc.

Incredible Creatures of the Caribbean Sea is a revision of *Water Planet: Life in the Caribbean Sea*, originally published in 2018 by Purple Toad Publishing, Inc. Reproduction of its contents is strictly prohibited without written permission from the rights holder.

Paperback ISBN 979-8-89094-178-7
Hardcover ISBN 979-8-89094-179-4

Library of Congress Control Number: 2024950034

To learn more about the other great books from Fox Chapel Publishing, or to find a retailer near you, call toll-free at 800-457-9112 or visit us at *www.FoxChapelPublishing.com*.
You can also send mail to:
Fox Chapel Publishing
903 Square Street
Mount Joy, PA 17552

We are always looking for talented authors. To submit an idea, please send a brief inquiry to acquisitions@foxchapelpublishing.com.

Fox Chapel Publishing makes every effort to use environmentally friendly paper for printing.

Printed in China